"I've been doing this since I was 12. . . . I honestly never expected things to get as big as they did. . . . It just got crazy."

JUSTIN TIMBERLAKE to *USA Today*

For my father, Richard, and daughter, Eva, and the love of music that keeps them forever young.

Photographs © 2009: Alamy Images/Jack Carey: 28; **AP Images/**Jason DeCrow: 6 left; **Corbis Images:** 67 (Mario Anzuoni/Reuters), 21, 52, 53 (T. Beckwith/New York Post/Sygma), 30 (Tibor Bozi), 40, 102 center left (Michael Lewis), 62 (Pacha), 64, 65 (Reuters), 43, 102 bottom left (Marko Shark), 56, 57 (Frank Trapper/Sygma); **Everett Collection, Inc.:** 2 (Steve Fenn/ABC), 88 (NBC), 89 (Paramount), 24; **Getty Images:** 32 (Dave Allocca), 36, 39 main, 46 (Bob Berg), 77 (Lisa Blumen-feld), 81 (Chad Buchanan), 37 (Bill Davila), 99 (Fred Duval), 22 (Don Emmert), 42 (Steve Granitz), 10 (Scott Gries), 63, 49, 102 top right (Scott Harrison), 16 (Gavin Hellier), 82 (Dave Hogan), 97 (Chris Jackson), 85 (Glenn James), 8, 9 (Dimitrios Kambouris), 83 (MJ Kim), 72 (Peter Kramer), 44 (Andy Lyons), 51, 103 bottom right (Jeffrey Mayer), 3, 7 right, 11, 74, 94 (Kevin Mazur), 27, 34, 50 (Frank Micelotta), 68, 73 (Tim Mosenfelder), 58 (Lucy Nicholson), 91 (Albert L. Ortega), 70 (Jeff Vespa), 1 (Kevin Winter); **Landov, LLC:** 18 (Fitzroy Barrett), 60 (Ezio Petersen/UPI), 86 (Photopro); **NEWSCOM:** 7 left, 61; **Retna Ltd.:** 92 (Sebastian Artz), 6 right, 17 (Bill Davila), cover (Sara DeBoer), 78, 84 (Armando Gallo), 12 (Bernhard Kuhmstedt), 14 (Andrew Marks), back cover (John Spellman); **ShutterStock, Inc.:** 29 (Linda Bucklin), 90 (Bonita R. Chesier), 102 center right (Marc Dietrich), 95 (Dole), 102 top left (HomeStudio), 39 inset (Patsy A. Jacks), 96 (Jasna), 55 bottom (konstantynov), 103 top (Obak), 54 (Thomas M. Perkins), 19 (Michael Pettigrew), 48 (Larry Powell), 103 bottom left (ultimathule), 76 (Silvio Verrecchia), 102 bottom right (Graca Victoria); **Splash News:** 33 (Toby Canham), 15, 55 top

Library of Congress Cataloging-in-Publication Data
Dougherty, Steve, 1948–
  Justin Timberlake / Steven Dougherty.
    p. cm. — (Junk food: tasty celebrity bios)
  Includes bibliographical references, discography, and index.
  Library/Book Clubs/Trade ISBN-10: 0-531-23700-1
  ISBN-13: 978-0-531-23700-7
  Book Fairs ISBN-10: 0-531-23401-0
  ISBN-13: 978-0-531-23401-3

  1. Timberlake, Justin, 1981—Juvenile literature. 2. Singers—United States—Biography—Juvenile literature. I. Title.
  ML3930.T58D67 2009   782.42164092—dc22   [B]   2008028313

SCHOLASTIC, FRANKLIN WATTS, and associated logos are trademarks and/or registered trademarks of Scholastic Inc.

1 2 3 4 5 6 7 8 9 10 R 18 17 16 15 14 16 12 11 10 09

Justin
TIMBERLAKE

BY
STEVE DOUGHERTY

Franklin Watts®
An Imprint of Scholastic Inc.

WITH FAMILY
page 17

IN 'NSYNC
page 61

IN HOLLYWOOD
page 94

★ JUNK FOOD

STAR GUiDE

LARGER THAN LIFE:
Justin introduces a fellow pop phenomenon—Madonna.

CRAZY FOR YOU

How sweet it is! It's March 10, 2008, and Justin Timberlake is about to introduce Madonna, one of his all-time favorite singers, at the Rock and Roll Hall of Fame banquet in New York. Excited as he is about the honor, he has to be nervous. The audience in the ballroom of the posh Waldorf-Astoria hotel is full of legendary rock stars like Billy Joel and John Mellencamp. Justin, who just turned 27, has been listening to their music all his life.

Justin knows it's a huge honor to introduce Madonna—the most successful female singer in the history of pop music. So when Madonna walks to the stage, Justin drops to his knees and bows before the Queen of Pop.

HUGE HONOR: Justin inducts Madonna into the Rock and Roll Hall of Fame.

It is such an unexpected gesture that Madonna and everyone in the audience looks surprised. Then the whole crowd breaks into applause. One thing is clear: Justin Timberlake, former boy-band phenom, has earned the respect of the biggest names in rock 'n' roll.

In case you were wondering, Justin will be a lock for the

Hall himself in 2023, 25 years after he rocketed to fame with 'NSync in 1998.

So it's hard to believe that not so long ago, Justin was just another kid who felt he didn't fit in. He never dreamed that one day he might take his place alongside his heroes in pop music's hall of fame.

STRONG TIES: Justin, age 15, with his mom, Lynn. "My mom always said to me, 'If you're gonna do it, don't do it halfway. You've got to give 150 percent,'" Justin recalls.

a SUPERSTAR iS BORN

Justin grows up in a world filled with music.

Justin Randall Timberlake was born in Memphis, Tennessee, a thousand miles from the ballrooms of New York City. It was January 31, 1981. Madonna was two years away from releasing her first album, and no one had any idea that baby Justin would eventually be hanging with the legends of pop music. But it wasn't hard to guess that music would play a big part in his life.

MUSICAL ROOTS

Growing up in nearby Millington, Tennessee, Justin was surrounded by musicians. His father, Randy Timberlake, played bass and sang in a bluegrass band. He also directed the church choir.

One of Justin's grandfathers, Bill Bomar, played a mean guitar. He taught his grandson how to play as soon as Justin was big enough to hold the instrument.

DiD YOU KNOW?

JUSTIN IS OFTEN PHOTOGRAPHED WEARING A SUN STUDIO T-SHIRT in honor of the Memphis recording studio where the King of Rock 'n' Roll, Elvis Presley, began his career. (See page 12.)

According to family legend, Bill used to play in informal jam sessions with the King of Rock 'n' Roll, Elvis Presley. When Justin got older, his

FAMILY GUY: Justin escorts his grandparents to the opening of his New York City barbecue restaurant.

14

grandfather gave him the guitar that he had used when he played with Elvis.

BaBY'S GOT BeaT

FATHER AND SONS: Justin poses with his half brother Jonathan and his father, Randy, in 2003.

Justin's mother, Lynn Harless, sang and loved all kinds of music. "When Justin was a little-bitty baby," she told *Rolling Stone* magazine, "we'd sit him . . . on the kitchen counter. He'd kick his legs to the beat of the music. We'd change the music and he'd kick to the new beat!"

According to Randy Timberlake, Justin loved to perform from day one. "We never had to teach him to sing," Randy told a reporter for the *Sun* in London. "Even as a toddler, he would sing and dance for us. When he was just two or three, he would jump onstage when my band was playing and pretend to play his toy guitar."

Luckily for Justin, he had a music-lover's paradise right down the road while he was growing up. Millington is just nine miles from Memphis, the birthplace of rock 'n' roll. In the 1950s, people flocked to the clubs on the city's legendary Beale Street. There they listened to the music of blues guitarist B.B. King, the deep voice of country star Johnny Cash, and the rocking piano wizardry of Jerry Lee Lewis. If they were lucky, they got to see Justin's grandfather's friend, Elvis Presley.

Years later, when Justin was in his teens, the city was still alive with good music. He remembers walking down Beale Street and

DID YOU KNOW?

TENNESSEE IS FAMOUS FOR NOT ONE BUT TWO MUSIC CAPITALS. Memphis is known as the Blues Capital; Nashville is called the Capital of Country Music.

MUSIC MECCA: As a teen, Justin came to Memphis to soak up the city's famous R&B.

soaking up the powerful sounds of rhythm-and-blues and soul that poured out of the clubs.

KEY CHANGE

By the time Justin was old enough to appreciate the music on Beale Street, however, his family life had changed forever. When he was three, his parents divorced. An only child, Justin continued to live with his mother while his father moved to another house in Millington and later remarried. His beloved "Granny," Sadie Bomar, lived next door and helped raise Justin after Randy left. "The divorce was hard on Justin," Sadie told the *Sun* of London. "It's a very confusing thing for a boy. . . . He couldn't understand why [his dad] wasn't there for him anymore."

As much as he missed his father, Justin soon had a stepfather in his life. Lynn

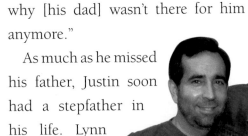

ALL IN THE FAMILY: Justin hugs his mom, Lynn, and his stepfather, Paul Harless.

married Paul Harless, a local banker, when Justin was five.

Justin also had a best friend he could count on for support. Trace Ayala and Justin met when they were babies, and their mothers were best friends. The two boys were born months apart, and they grew up in houses just a few blocks from each other.

TALENTED BUT TORTURED

When Justin started elementary school, he got good grades, and it quickly became clear that he was talented and athletic. He loved playing basketball after school, and he excelled at video games. On his bedroom wall at home, he hung posters of his music idol, Michael Jackson, and basketball genius Michael Jordan.

Justin loved to dance around the house and sing to his parents'

BEST BUDS: Justin and lifelong friend Trace Ayala grew up near each other.

Michael Jackson and Stevie Wonder albums. He entertained his family by telling jokes and dancing at Christmas and other holidays. He was full of mischief, but he was also well-mannered and polite.

Justin also had his quiet moments. He was shy around other people and kept to himself. Sometimes he felt an anger that he just couldn't explain. "I was a tortured young dude—to the point of rage," Justin told *Rolling Stone*.

BAD HAIR DAYS

In public, Justin spent a lot of time scowling and staring at his feet. "My mom makes jokes. She says, 'It's no shock to me you're obsessed with sneakers because that's the only thing you looked at for the first ten years of your life.'"

What's more, Justin says, he couldn't stand to look at himself in the mirror. "I had really awkward hair and terrible skin, and I was really scrawny," Justin told GMTV, Europe's music TV network. "I was a really weird-looking kid!"

T or F ?

Justin hates animals.

FALSE! When Justin was growing up, he had dogs named Scooter and Ollie and cats named Millie and Alley!

19

On the playground, kids called Justin "Pizza Face" and "Curly" and "Brillo." "I hated my hair," Justin told the Associated Press. "That was the thing everybody teased me about. In second grade, I took school scissors and just cut my hair all uneven. I was like, 'I can't stand this!'"

His mom's reaction? "That's the only time I ever really got [in big trouble]," Justin remembered.

BRiLLO GOeS OnSTaGe

Kids in school even made fun of Justin for something he did really well—singing. But all the teasing in the world couldn't keep Justin away from the stage. In 1989, just a year after he hacked off his hair with a pair of dull scissors, Justin entered a talent show at the E.E. Jeter Elementary School. Few of the students, teachers, and parents on hand could have expected

YIKES!
Meet "Brillo," age 19. Yep, that's the hair that humiliated Justin!

much from the shy and awkward eight-year-old everyone called Brillo.

One person in the audience, however, guessed what was coming. Justin's mother, Lynn, brought a video camera to tape the performance.

Justin and four friends were planning to perform a New Kids on the Block song. At the time, the New Kids were the biggest pop act in America. Justin's group had decided to dance to one of their songs and mouth the words.

But when the curtain went up, Justin didn't lip-synch along with the rest. Instead he sang the lead vocal part in a strong and clear voice.

The audience went wild. Justin's mom recorded it all with her video camera— including the wildly enthusiastic reaction of the crowd.

> I grew up listening to country music. My grandfather taught me about Johnny Cash and Willie Nelson and the importance that they had.
>
> **JUSTIN** to *Rolling Stone* magazine

Having "it"

Justin knew from day one that he wanted to be a performer. He had already been begging his mom to get him singing lessons. After the talent show, she took the videotape to a voice teacher named Bob Westbrook. "Justin loved the stage back then, and he had that charisma," Bob later told a reporter for the *Memphis Commercial Appeal*. "You either have it or you don't."

Justin soaked up everything Bob could tell him about vocal technique. Just a couple of years after Justin started singing lessons, the ten-year-old entered

T or F

?

Justin Timberlake appeared on *Star Search* when he was 11.

FALSE! JT entered the contest as Justin Randall. After he lost, he never used that stage name again.

a contest at the legendary Grand Ole Opry in Nashville, Tennessee. Justin's performance amazed the judges, and they awarded him first prize—$16,000.

Soon after, Lynn heard that the popular TV talent show *Star Search* was looking for young performers. So she and Justin drove all the way to Orlando, Florida, to audition. He sang for the show's producers— and they invited him to compete on national TV.

Would this be Justin's big break?

anD THE WinnER iS...

For his first TV appearance— which you can still find on YouTube—Justin sang a country song. He wore a ten-gallon hat and showed off his dance moves. But when the winner was announced, it was the girl he was competing against who jumped for joy.

Justin was gracious in defeat.* But he was crushed. He had gotten his big chance—and blown it. There was no reason to believe that he would ever get that kind of exposure again.

FAST BREAK: Landing a role on the *New Mickey Mouse Club* was the big break Justin had been looking for.

2

THE MOUSE THAT ROARED

Justin joins a very exclusive club— the *New Mickey Mouse Club*.

As disappointing as it was for Justin, losing out on *Star Search* turned out to be a blessing in disguise. Neither he nor his mom knew it, but a casting director from the Disney Channel's hit show, the *New Mickey Mouse Club*, had been in the audience during Justin's performance. He introduced himself to Lynn and suggested that her son audition for the popular after-school show.

Like *Star Search*, the *New Mickey Mouse Club* was

DID YOU KNOW?

JUSTIN AND BRITNEY BECAME GOOD FRIENDS ALMOST AS SOON AS THEY BEGAN REHEARSALS FOR THE *NEW MICKEY MOUSE CLUB.*

"They have a lot in common," the show's casting director told *People*. "They certainly share the same interests—singing, dancing, acting."

produced in Orlando. Lynn and Justin left the *Star Search* studio and went straight to the tryouts. If he had won his round in the *Star Search* competition, he never would have made it in time for his audition.

BiG BReaK

Disney's original *Mickey Mouse Club* was a black-and-white afternoon variety show. Justin's parents had loved watching it when they were kids in the 1950s. And Justin was a fan of the new show, which Disney brought back in 1989. "I remember seeing the show on TV and thinking, 'Man, what an incredible experience that must be!'" Justin later told a reporter on ABC News' *20/20*.

Before long, he got a chance to find out. Justin wowed the Mouse Club judges, and out of 20,000 kids, Justin was one of 20 chosen for the show. Forget about *Star Search*. Justin had his big break.

Joining the cast meant big changes for Justin. Each season

lasted for six months, so Justin and his mom left their home in Tennessee and moved to Orlando.

iN GOOD COMPANY

When Justin arrived at MGM Studios, he found that he was one of the youngest kids in the cast. But he was in good company. Two other talented 11-year-olds joined the group that year: Britney Spears and Christina Aguilera.

The oldest cast member was JC Chasez, who had been on the show for two years already. JC and Justin immediately hit it off and became close friends. "I love his sincerity," JC later told *TV Hits* magazine.

OVERHEARD

We used to joke around backstage and say, "Whenever the show ends, we'll all go off our separate ways and become stars!"

CHRISTINA AGUILERA
to *USA Today*

CLASS ACT: Justin takes a time-out to chat with some fans in London, England.

"Justin is a really nice, genuine kind of person."

A typical day for Justin began at 6 A.M. After breakfast, a Disney bus picked him up and drove him to school—in a special classroom on the studio lot. After three hours of schoolwork, Justin rehearsed all afternoon. Then it took three hours to film each episode before a live audience. Like any middle school student, Justin still had to do his homework when his day was done.

Justin loved working on the show because he got to act, dance, and sing. "You get to dip your fingers into everything," JT told *All-Stars*. "You're not restricted to one thing at all. Doing the comedy was a lot of fun."

T or F ?

Britney and Justin acted like spoiled brats on the set of the *New Mickey Mouse Club*.

FALSE! "They both were incredibly polite kids," the casting director said.

Justin was having the time of his life. And then it all came to an end. Without warning, Disney canceled the show in February 1995, just after Justin turned 14. What a lousy birthday present!

MERE MORTAL:
In 1995, Justin moved back home—and out of show business.

BACK TO EARTH

Justin feels out of sync back home in Tennessee, until a phone call changes his life.

After the dream-come-true-excitement of the *New Mickey Mouse Club*, Justin moved back to Millington in 1995 and returned to school. He had a hard time adjusting to life as an ordinary teenager. "I got so bored and really down about everything," he told *Teen People*. "I wasn't focusing like I could. I didn't have the inspiration that music gave me."

Finally one day, he just broke down and cried. "Luckily, my mom was there and said, 'Think about this. If show business is taking such a toll, is this something you really want to do?'" Justin thought about it—and realized that the answer was yes. He wanted a life in show business more than anything. He told *Teen People*, "That's my place in the world. That's where I belong."

MOROSE iN MiLLiNGTON

Justin didn't see how finishing high school was going to help him get back into show business. But his mom wasn't about to let him drop out of school and sing on street corners. Lynn told TV journalist Barbara Walters that she said to her son, "You're going to finish high school if we have to go handcuffed together!"

So Justin stuck it out. In Millington, it would have been easy for him to act like a big deal in a small town. But his friends and family helped him keep it real. He and his best friend from childhood, Trace Ayala, spent a lot of time together. And his mom and stepdad, Paul, made sure Justin kept his feet on the ground.

When Justin begged to get his ears pierced, Paul told him it was a

SCHOOL DAYS: "I was good with all the teachers and principals, so I never got in trouble," Justin told *Tiger Beat*.

BIG BROTHER: Justin pays a visit to his half brothers, Stephen (right) and Jonathan (left). They're with Justin's dad, Randy, and his stepmother, Lisa.

THE FUTURE OF POP:
Justin opens a tour in
San Diego in 2008.

T or F

?

Justin trained
for years
to learn to be
such a fantastic
dancer.

He had very little
dance training.

FALSE!

34

privilege that had to be earned. To earn that privilege, Justin had to write a song and perform it for the family. Justin was up to the task. He wrote a ditty called "The Earring Song" and sang it during a family vacation in Hawai'i. As soon as he returned home, Justin went to a Memphis mall and got both ears pierced.

Back in Business

Then in the summer of 1995, following his freshman year in high school, Justin got a telephone call that changed his life.

The call came from Chris Kirkpatrick, a singer Justin had been friends with in Orlando. Chris was ten years older than Justin and sang in a 1950s-style vocal group, the Hollywood High Tones, at a Universal Studios theme park. He wanted to know whether Justin was interested in helping him form a new vocal group.

Was he ever!

Chris explained that he had tried out for another group, the Backstreet Boys, who were already on their way to pop stardom. Chris didn't win a spot with the Boys, but the group's manager, Lou Pearlman, wanted him to start up a second five-member group. Chris had told Pearlman about Justin, and they had agreed that Justin should fly to Orlando for an audition.

After he got off the phone with Chris, Justin talked the idea over with his mother. That same day, they flew to Orlando.

iT ALL COMES TOGETHER

There's nothing wrong with aiming for the stars!

JUSTIN

At age 14, Justin was already an accomplished performer who knew how to connect with an audience. Pearlman was so impressed by Justin's audition that he invited him to join the group right away. Pearlman realized he could build his new five-member group around the talented, blue-eyed singer.

Justin, in turn, encouraged Pearlman to recruit JT's former Mouse mate JC Chasez. Soon, another Universal theme-park performer, Joey Fatone, signed on. The last member to join was Lance Bass, a Memphis singer who had been recommended by Justin's voice coach, Bob Westbrook.

Because Justin was only

DEN MOTHER: Justin's mom, Lynn Harless, moved to Orlando to watch over Justin and his 'NSync band mates.

14, Pearlman hired tutors to coach him in his schoolwork. Justin's mom, Lynn, moved to Orlando so she could be there for her underage son. Because she lived in the house Pearlman rented for the boys, she became "den mother" for the whole band.

The boys started rehearsing and working with voice coaches to perfect their complicated five-part vocal harmonies. They also had choreographers to help them develop the dance routines that would become a signature part of their act.

After months of hard work, the group was beginning to come together. They recorded a two-song demo, and Pearlman started sending it out to record companies. The band finally felt they were ready to perform in public. There was just one minor problem: The group had no name.

GETTING IN SYNC

Once again, Justin's mom came to the rescue. One night after rehearsals, the five band members had dinner with Lynn and Paul. Lynn began talking about how the group's harmonies sounded so tight and the boys seemed "very much in sync" with each other.

With a tiny spelling change, 'NSync was born.

FULL MOON! Before he joined 'NSync, Joey Fatone had a gig performing in a wacky musical in Orlando—dressed as a werewolf.

And just in time. Pearlman had been having trouble getting a major record company to sign the boys, but he had finally gotten them a deal—with a company in Germany. The manager told the members of the newly minted 'NSync to get their passports ready. They were going to Europe.

In January 1996, as Justin turned 15, he found himself on a plane to Europe with his new band mates. As he flew across the Atlantic Ocean, Justin knew there was no good reason to believe that sophisticated European audiences would take an interest in them. After all, they'd been rejected by every major label in the United States—and they didn't even have a CD in the stores or a song on the radio!

READY TO ROLL! Europe was about to be bowled over by the biggest boy band ever to hit the scene.

BLAST OFF!

Justin and his 'NSync band mates conquer the Old World.

From sunny Florida, Justin and his band mates flew to Stockholm, Sweden, a city near the Arctic Circle where the sun shines just a few hours a day during the winter. But despite the darkness and the cold, the members of 'NSync worked hard in the beginning of 1996 to record songs for their first album.

In October 1996, they released the group's first single, "I Want You Back," in Germany. It became a hit almost from the day it aired on the radio. The song got so much radio play that the group's very first performances were sold out. On their first-ever tour, 'NSync performed more than 30

OVERHEARD!

When we put our band together, I didn't even know who the Backstreet Boys were.

JUSTIN to *Teen People*

FACE OF THE BAND: Justin performs at the Forum in Los Angeles in 1999.

concerts in a single month. And at practically every stop on the tour, they were mobbed by screaming fans as soon as they stepped off their bus.

For Justin and the other members of 'NSync, success came so fast it was bewildering. One minute they were a group of lonely Americans far from home. The next minute, they were teen idols who had to fight their way to the stage through crowds of screaming fans. Because Justin usually sang the lead, he became the focus of attention. Before long, he couldn't leave his hotel room without being chased down the street. Eventually, he and the other band members had to have bodyguards to protect them whenever they were out in public.

> We're nothing but happy, and we love our fans!
>
> **JUSTIN**
> to *16* magazine

DID YOU KNOW?

THE BACKSTREET BOYS WERE ONE OF THE MOST POPULAR ALL-GUY GROUPS IN THE WORLD—**until 'NSync came along and sold more albums and became even more popular.**

By early 1997, the group's first album, *NSync*, had sold more than 250,000 copies in Germany alone, an amazing accomplishment for an unknown group from the U.S.

With two more hit songs on the radio—"Tearin' Up My Heart" and "Here We Go"—the first 'NSync album became a hit throughout Europe. As the group's fame spread, Pearlman extended the tour to England, Scandinavia, Poland, Hungary, and as far away as South Africa.

By the end of 1997, people all over the world knew the band members by name. But back in the good old U.S.A., they were complete unknowns.

Then a scout for RCA Records, one of the biggest record labels in America, caught an 'NSync concert in Budapest, Hungary.

DID YOU KNOW?

JUSTIN'S BAND MATES HAD LOTS OF NICKNAMES FOR HIM. They called the youngest member of the group Curly, The Baby, Mr. Smooth, and Bounce—the last name inspired by his love for basketball.

44

Within a few months, the group was signed to RCA, the same label that had made Elvis Presley a star.

After spending almost two years in Europe and touring the world, Justin, JC, Joey, Chris, and Lance flew back home in time for the spring 1998 U.S. release of their debut album.

HOMEWARD BOUND

Excited as he was, Justin was full of doubts. Would American audiences embrace them the way fans in Europe and around the world had? Justin wasn't sure. "We certainly didn't expect things to go as well as they did in Europe," Justin later told *Billboard* magazine. At best, he added, he expected the group "to have half as much success in the U.S."

BACK IN THE U.S.A.: In 1998, Justin and 'NSync made a triumphant return to the States when they won two Billboard Video Music Awards for their hit "I Want You Back."

ON TOP OF THE WORLD

Justin finds success can be dizzying— and fleeting.

In Europe, Justin couldn't walk down the street without being chased by fans—usually (big surprise!) girls. Back home, no one knew him from Adam. Or Joey or JC for that matter.

That changed in the spring of 1998 when "I Want You Back" was first played on the radio in America. The single shot straight up the *Billboard* magazine charts. At the same time, an exciting new video for the song appeared on MTV. Fans wanted to learn everything they could about the group—especially the lead singer with the smooth moves and sweet voice.

On March 24, 1998, the group released their debut album, *NSync, in the U.S. To promote it, Justin and the boys performed mini concerts in radio stations and even in shopping malls. Imagine the surprise of mall cruisers spotting JT moonwalking in front of the food court!

THE WiLD RiDE BEGiNS

'NSync's big break came when they performed on Disney's nationally televised Summer Concert series. It turned millions of TV viewers into 'NSync fans overnight. After that, no shopping mall in the world was big enough for an 'NSync show.

Then Janet Jackson, sister of Justin's music idol, Michael Jackson, invited 'NSync to be the opening act for her *Velvet Rope* tour. Justin and his band mates were thrilled.

'NSync toured with Janet Jackson for a few weeks in October 1998. But it soon became obvious that 'NSync was

T or F
?
Some fans lived in a dumpster for a week to win tickets to an 'NSync concert.

TRUE! It was a contest. And the winners came out smelling like roses!

HEADLINERS: 'NSync salutes their fans at a concert in Las Vegas.

too popular to open for other artists. It was time for the guys to launch their own U.S. tour.

Knowing he was going to be away from home for a long time, Justin invited his best friend, Trace Ayala, to travel with him and the group. JT and Trace had been through a lot together growing up. Now they were about to share a wilder ride than either of them ever imagined.

To join them on tour, 'NSync chose Justin's former Mouse Club friend, Britney Spears. At the time, Britney was still unknown. The group introduced her to their audience just as Janet Jackson had introduced 'NSync to hers.

For Justin, who was reunited with Britney four years after

SETTING THE STAGE: Justin performs at the Grammy Awards in L.A. in 2002. He would later win his own Grammys in 2004 and 2008.

Disney closed the Mouse Club, it was love at first—or second—sight. "My head spun!" Justin told *People*.

When Britney's song, "Baby, One More Time," became a huge hit, the two teen idols became one of pop music's most glamorous and successful couples. Britney then left the 'NSync tour to perform as the star of her own concert tour—but she and Justin saw each other every chance they could. And when their schedules made that impossible, they kept their relationship strong by talking on the phone three or four times a day.

STRAIGHT TO THE TOP

For Justin, 'NSync's success was almost unbelievable. When he found out that the group's first album was the second-best-selling album in America, it "was a little overwhelming," he told *Billboard*. "I was jumping up and down. I didn't know what to say!"

Before long, Justin was

THE FIRST COUPLE OF POP:
Justin and Britney wore matching outfits to the American Music Awards in 2001.

getting 500 letters a day from fans all over the world. But he barely had time to read his mail. He was on the road for most of the year, playing more than 100 concerts in 1998.

By the end of year, the group's debut album had sold seven million copies, and fans were lining up to buy their second album, *Home for Christmas*.

On THE ROAD again

By the time they launched their 1999 tour, 'NSync was the hottest new group in pop music. Justin and his band mates found themselves pictured on boxes of Kellogg's Corn Pops cereal. They even appeared on postage stamps issued by the Caribbean island nation of St. Vincent and the Grenadines.

When the boys went on the road, they traveled in tour buses equipped with extra bunk beds to fit friends and family. During the long drives between concert sites, the five group members sat on big couches, playing video games and watching DVDs.

BOY WONDERS: From left are 'NSync stars JC Chasez, Joey Fatone, Chris Kirkpatrick, Lance Bass, and Justin Timberlake.

To know that you've touched them enough that they know [all your songs] by heart—that's special!

JUSTIN on his fans, to *Bop* magazine

Justin and his band mates often arrived at concert sites early in the morning. To kill time between soundchecks, "meet-and-greets" with fans, and interviews with the local press, they rode bicycles and played video games together backstage.

OVERHEARD

T or F

Justin is an excellent cook.

FALSE!
"I can make a really mean Pop Tart and a nice bowl of cereal," Justin joked to an interviewer in England. "I'm exceptional at browning toast!"

When Justin wanted time to himself, he liked to find a berth on the bus, light candles, and meditate. "I sit on my bed, close my eyes, breathe deeply and get into a zone," he told *Rolling Stone*. "You get that moment where you block everything out, and you just feel, and it takes you to a whole other place. It's kinda like my conversation with God."

The bigger the group got, the closer the five members of 'NSync grew to one another. "We're not just a recording group," Justin told *Billboard*. "We're friends. We're growing and changing and making music that is real and honest."

Ka-CHiNG!

They were also making a ton of money. Justin spent his on things that he loved—cars and shoes. He began a collection of vehicles that would grow to include three Mercedes, two Cadillac Escalades, an Audi TT, a Dodge Viper, a BMW, a Porsche, five motorcycles, not to

FORTRESS OF SOLITUDE: Justin escaped the pressures of fame at his mansion in Orlando, Florida.

mention several Sea-Doo jet skis. To park his fleet, he bought a three-bedroom home in Orlando.

Justin fed his addiction to footwear by buying more than 450 pairs of boots and sneakers, including every edition of Air Jordans on the market.

YIKES! "I collect all kinds of sneakers. I have about 170 pairs. And they all smell!" Justin says.

On rare days when 'NSync wasn't on the road, Justin retreated to his "Fun Zone," a playroom in his Orlando house equipped with a pinball machine, an Xbox, and a PlayStation.

Near the end of 1999, 'NSync was on top of the world—and that was exactly when their first crisis hit. The band had become a big business. Their concert tour had sold more than $44 million worth of tickets. The sales of T-shirts, posters and other merchandise, as well as CDs, brought in many millions more. But where was all that money going?

BeTRaYeD

Although Justin and his band mates had more money than they had ever dreamed of, they had actually received only a fraction of what they had earned. The group members and their families studied 'NSync's finances. They decided that their manager, Lou Pearlman, had been keeping most of the profits for himself.

When the band members asked Pearlman to give them a fairer contract, he refused. Negotiations quickly broke down, and 'NSync decided to leave RCA and sign with Jive Records.

Pearlman promptly sued the band for breach of contract and demanded that they pay him a whopping $150 million! He also insisted that they stop recording and stop touring as 'NSync.

"He wasn't just suing us for $150 million," Justin told one interviewer. "He was suing us for our name."

SHOWDOWN

In December 1999, Pearlman and the 'NSync guys were about to have their showdown in court. After all the success he'd had in the past three years, Justin felt like he had hit rock bottom. "It was horrible," he told *Face* magazine. "It's the one time I honestly said, 'I don't want to do this anymore.' I thought our careers were over!"

You **have to** keep your family close.... All of my family [is] so proud of me. But I'm still... just that little kid who used to run around and act like a little smart aleck.

JUSTIN to the *Memphis Commercial Appeal*

THE STAR: Justin arrives at the Grammy Awards in 2002 to perform with 'NSync.

BiGGER and BeTTeR

Heading out on their own, Justin and 'NSync strike it rich—but success has its own costs.

Just when Justin was ready to hang it up, 'NSync's legal battle ended. Pearlman backed off and settled the suit out of court. Without admitting any wrongdoing, he agreed to let the group out of its contracts.

In January 2000, as Justin turned 19, 'NSync was back on track. The group released its first single with Jive Records. The song "Bye Bye Bye" had special meaning for Justin and his band mates—not just because it hit No. 1 on the charts and was eventually named one of *Rolling Stone*'s and MTV's "100 Greatest Pop Songs" in history. It was special because it served as the group's good-bye to Lou Pearlman.

If their former manager and producer didn't get the message when "Bye Bye Bye" came out, he surely did when he saw the title of 'NSync's new album: *No Strings Attached*.

NO STRiNGS aTTaCHED

The new album served as the group's declaration of independence. On the cover, Justin and the rest of the group appear as puppets breaking free of a puppeteer.

And if Pearlman thought that the band would be lost without his guiding hand, he was wrong. The new album sold faster than any other album in history. In just

When Justin had curly hair, we'd joke around with him, like, "Uh oh! Curl No. 66 is out of place!" He wants to make sure he looks good.

LANCE BASS to *People* magazine

OVERHEARD

60

TAKING THEIR CHANCES: The success of 'NSync's *No Strings Attached* indicated that the band would do just fine without their first manager.

ten hours, fans scooped up one million copies. In all, it would sell more than 15 million copies.

BRANCHING OUT

No Strings Attached was a big change from the bubblegum pop of 'NSync's first two albums. "This album is more diverse, a little edgier," Justin told *Teen* magazine. "It's a little more mature, but we're still gonna keep the harmonies because that's really our sound."

Justin was especially proud because one song on the album, "I'll Be Good For You," was co-written by none other than . . .

Justin Timberlake. "The coolest thing about songwriting," Justin told one reporter, "is to know it started with this little guitar riff, and the next thing you know, it's being played on the radio."

JUSTiN'S POP ODYSSeY

To promote the album (as if they needed to), 'NSync embarked on one of the most ambitious and successful concert tours ever. The band members' 2001 *PopOdyssey* tour was bigger and better than any previous 'NSync tour.

Tickets to the shows sold out almost as soon as they went on sale. Fans lucky enough to see the act were dazzled. The dance numbers were acrobatic and athletic. And the lights and costumes lifted the show to a new level. For one song, the five singers appeared onstage dressed like astronauts in silver space suits.

SONGWRITER: 'NSync's *Celebrity*, with six songs written by Justin, became the second-fastest-selling record in pop music history.

The success of their new music put more focus than ever on Justin. In 2000, the 19-year-old came in first in *People* magazine's online poll of "The Most Beautiful People in the World," edging out his girlfriend, Britney.

By the time 'NSync went into the studio to record their next album, *Celebrity*, Justin was the undisputed leader of the group. "He's restless, driven, polite, and pleasant," *Rolling Stone* reported in a profile of the band in 2001.

In the studio, Justin took on an ever-greater role. He helped produce five of the songs on *Celebrity* and co-wrote six of the tracks, including the smash hits "Pop" and "Gone."

TiMe TO CHiLL

For all his success, however, Justin struggled with the demands of fame. After five years in the spotlight, the constant cycle of recording and touring was wearing on him. Privacy was in short supply. "It's very hard to find your own peace and quiet," Justin said in an AOL interview.

To escape the pressure and maintain his sanity, Justin took up

GAGA OVER GOLF: Justin finds that golf is a great way to relax.

FLYING HIGH: 'NSync performs at a sold-out concert in Las Vegas, during their smash hit tour for *No Strings Attached*.

golf. "Playing golf, you're in one place for four or five hours," he told journalist Sean Smith. "I can be myself."

HearTBreak

During 'NSync's long tours, Justin often felt homesick. Justin's half brothers, Jonathan and Stephen, were eight and three and growing fast. "I hardly ever see them anymore," Justin said. "Sometimes it makes me sad because every time I go home, my brothers have grown another foot taller."

Justin also felt physically run-down. Living on hotel food and backstage buffets took its toll, and he suffered from exhaustion and chronic bouts of flu.

And touring had an even more painful side effect than health problems: Heartache.

Justin's relationship with Britney was his first serious romance. He even talked about settling down with her and starting a family. "We'd both like to have children," Justin said in an interview with *The People* in London. "I've always wanted a big family. A whole basketball team would be good!" he joked.

Britney's second big hit, "Oops . . . I Did It Again," made her one of the biggest stars in pop music. With both performers touring separately, it became harder and harder for them to spend time together. As Justin's mom told *People* magazine, "You can't have a relationship when you see each other only two days a month."

ALWAYS ONSTAGE: Justin is mobbed by autograph seekers in 2006.

With the release of *Celebrity* in July 2001, things only got more hectic for Justin. The tour that followed was 'NSync's biggest and most extravagant ever. In the most famous production number, the five singers dropped from the sky, suspended on wires. The set was so elaborate it took 50 trucks and 24 buses to haul the crew and equipment around the country.

OUT OF SYNC

When the long and exhausting tour ended in April 2002, all five members were eager to find out what life was like beyond 'NSync. Lance Bass hoped to fulfill a lifelong dream of visiting outer space. Joey Fatone and Chris Kirkpatrick wanted to explore acting. JC Chasez wanted to record a solo album. And Justin had already written and recorded some tunes that he planned to include in his own solo album.

So, in the spring of 2002, the five members of 'NSync announced that, after seven years of almost nonstop performing, they were taking a break.

Neither they nor anyone else realized that they had just finished their final tour together.

POST-'NSYNC: After the breakup of 'NSync in the spring of 2002, Justin looked forward to a new chapter in his life.

THE new KiNG OF POP

Justin goes it alone—and rises straight to the top.

Justin was 21 years old. For the first time in his life, he was on his own. He was living in Orlando, far from his family in Tennessee. It was a good time to do some soul-searching. "I was 14 when ['NSync] started," he said in an interview. "I reached the point where I was growing up. I wanted to try something different."

For as long as he could remember, Justin had wanted to make a solo record. Finally, it seemed like the time to do it. "I had this music inside me and I knew it was something not everyone in the group would want to do," he told one reporter.

JUSTiN 2.0

With his band mates' blessing, Justin enlisted the Neptunes, the superstar duo that produced *Celebrity*, to help him with the album. He also partnered with Tim Mosely, the hip-hop producer and drummer known as Timbaland.

The album provided Justin with at least one measure of how far he'd come since his days as a Mousketeer. He invited one of his lifelong music heroes, Stevie Wonder, to play harmonica on the ballad "Nothin' Else." "When Stevie came in to record it," Justin told an interviewer for *Cosmopolitan*, "I almost cried, just realizing that somebody like him is playing on a song I wrote!"

Justin's solo album, *Justified*, was unlike anything he had recorded with 'NSync. Fans got a taste of the new sound when he appeared solo for the first time at the 2002 MTV Video Music Awards. Justin sang "Like I Love You," a funky dance tune that wasn't quite as sweet as the love

Gossip Alert!

Amanda Bynes of *What I Like About You* told *People* magazine that JT is her ideal guy—because he's "so funny and so talented."

T or F ?

After he went solo, Justin said 'NSync's music was childish and fake.

FALSE!

"Everything we did was genuine!" he told *Interview* magazine.

SAYING GOOD-BYE: Justin performs one of his last sets with 'NSync, at the Compaq Center in San Jose, California, on March 8, 2002.

songs he sang with 'NSync.

With a new, edgier sound, Justin seemed to have hit another level of maturity. He'd co-written all 13 songs on *Justified*, and he was proud of the album. "This is different, not only from 'NSync, but from anything out there," he told *USA Today*. "It may take people a few listens to get it."

"CRY ME A RIVER"

It didn't take many listens to get "Cry Me A River," a song about a girl who cheats on her boyfriend. Most fans knew by then that JT and Britney had broken up after four years together. Rumor had it that Britney had been dating other guys. And when people saw the video, in which the girlfriend looked and dressed exactly like Britney, the meaning of the song seemed clear.

Justin wasn't shy about it. "Making [*Justified*] was almost like therapy," he told

Interview magazine. "I was dealing with so many things in my personal life at the time. You know, I have a little bit of a broken heart."

By the time the album was released, Justin had moved on. He was enjoying the single life. He went out a lot, dancing at clubs and hanging out with a wide circle of hip young musicians like John Mayer, the Black Eyed Peas, and Coldplay's Chris Martin.

a new Romance

Before long, the tabloids buzzed with rumors about Justin's love life. He reportedly dated *Charmed* star Alyssa Milano, actress and former 'NSync dancer Jenna Dewan, and former tour mates Janet Jackson and Christina Aguilera.

But Justin wasn't one to kiss and tell. "I haven't been with anyone," Justin insisted in an interview with *People*. "Not a date, not a kiss."

DID YOU KNOW?

'NSYNC FANS MAY BE SURPRISED TO KNOW WHO JT NAMES AS FAVORITE GROUPS: **Coldplay, the Strokes, the Killers, Arcade Fire, Radiohead.**

Then, in the spring of 2003, Justin did start dating someone: Cameron Diaz, whom he met at Nickelodeon's 2003 Kids' Choice Awards. Soon the paparazzi were following the couple everywhere they went. "I love what I do," Justin told *Rolling Stone*. "But I also love my privacy."

Justin spent most of 2003 on the road. In the spring, he toured to promote his solo album. In the summer, he co-headlined a hugely successful tour with his long-ago Mouseketeer buddy, Christina Aguilera.

OFF THE BeaTen PaTH

After many of the concerts, Justin left the arena and appeared un-announced in small clubs, where he would perform a full set of new material. Backed by a small rock band, he sat at the piano and sang. And he didn't dance once.

Justin began to feel a new kind of respect from his fans—and he loved

T or F ?

Justin is a big *American Idol* fan.

BOTH! He likes the show, but he doesn't like that "contestants are treated like cattle."

it. "It's liberating to walk out onstage and people [aren't] screaming just because you're standing there," he told *Rolling Stone*. "They're screaming because you did something to impress them. They don't put your poster on their wall—they just like your record."

By the end of 2003, Justin had won two Grammys and three MTV Video Music Awards. By February 2004, his solo album had sold more than three million copies. *Rolling Stone* magazine named him "the biggest pop star" of the year and crowned him "The New King of Pop."

For Justin, it couldn't possibly get better than this . . . right?

I like a confident girl. Not overwhelming, not sassy stuck-up types, but someone who knows herself and is comfortable with herself and has a good sense of humor.

JUSTIN to *Teen* magazine

OVERHEARD!

SILENCE: In 2004, Justin announced that he was taking time off from his music career.

SUPER POWERS

Justin conquers the pop world—but stumbles in matters of the heart. Even kings get tired now and then. After the newly crowned royal highness of pop released *Justified* and toured the world to promote it, he badly needed a break. "I just didn't have any creative juice left," he said in a *W* magazine interview.

To get his juices flowing again, Justin decided to take two years off from his music career. "That was amazing for me," he told *Rolling Stone*. "Just the little things, like sitting home on the weekend or . . . playing golf, then coming back home and calling it a day."

JUSTIN GOES HOLLYWOOD...

It wasn't all play and no work for Justin however. During his two-year "vacation," he started an acting career by making four movies. To get closer to the film scene, he moved to Los Angeles. He bought a huge Spanish-style mansion overlooking Sunset Boulevard in the heart of the Hollywood Hills. For companionship, he turned to the same person he did when he first left home to tour with 'NSync. Justin invited his best friend, Trace Alaya, to move west with him and be his roommate.

Conveniently, Justin's new house was close to Cameron's. When Justin wasn't making movies, he and Cameron liked to go snowboarding in the mountains or surfing in Hawai'i.

...BUT MUSIC PULLS HiM BACK

As much as Justin enjoyed his vacation from recording studios and tour buses, he missed his music. So, in the autumn of 2005, he called his friend Timbaland and got back to work.

On his new album, Justin once again co-wrote all the songs. Keyboard player Nate Hills told *Rolling Stone* that Justin never actually wrote down the lyrics. He just sang them as they popped into his head. "Everybody knows he's talented, but this dude wrote that whole album without touching a pen or paper," Hills said. "I've never heard of a singer doing that. I think it's some kind of super power!"

A year after he began work, Justin's album, *FutureSex/LoveSounds*, dropped. And when it did, it exploded. Critics who had dismissed Justin in the past wrote about him with new respect. They raved about his songwriting and the new,

NO WORRIES! Justin once said that his greatest fear was "to die unloved!" Nooo way will his fans let that happen!

TAKE A SECOND LOOK: These days Justin wants to be known more for his singing and composing than his dancing. Here, he performs in London in 2006.

emotional power of his singing. Many critics put JT's new CD on their "10 Best Albums of the Year" lists—not that fans needed anyone to tell them how good the album was. They bought 2.5 million copies, placing it fifth on the list of best-selling CDs for the year. *Future* spun off two No. 1 singles and earned Justin two Grammy Awards.

To celebrate his second solo album's success, JT toured Europe in 2006. Cameron came along for the ride.

The tour was a triumph, and Justin seemed as happy as he had ever been— in life and love. In December, when he appeared as the musical guest on *Saturday Night Live*, Cameron introduced him to the audience.

Weeks later, the couple abruptly announced in a statement to the press

> My first kiss was when I was ten, with my girlfriend. I was in sixth grade, and she was in eighth grade— I've always been into older women!
>
> **JUSTIN**

that after almost four years together, they had "ended [their] romantic relationship."

Justin and Cameron refused to say anything further about the breakup. But it was clear that Justin was devastated. "I'm a hopeless romantic," he told *People* magazine.

Justin didn't exactly sit around pining forever. After he and Cameron broke up, he reportedly dated some of Hollywood's most beautiful young actresses, including Kate Hudson and Scarlett Johansson. But even after JT and Jessica Biel were photographed snowboarding in Utah, Justin insisted that he still hadn't met Ms. Right. "I do still believe in love," Justin told one interviewer from *Marie Claire*. "It's out there . . . somewhere. It's the light at the end of the far, far tunnel!"

CAMERON ALERT: Sure, they *said* they broke up. But did the breakup stick?

WINNING TEAM: Justin with Dirk Nowitzki, the first European to be named the NBA's Most Valuable Player.

JUST ANOTHER SPORTS FAN?

When it comes to sports, Justin is a fanatic. His two favorites are golf and basketball. And whether he's on the fairway or on the hardwood, JT's got game!

Whenever Justin gets the chance, he likes to mix it up with the pros. In 2003, he wrote a new theme song for the NBA's TV broadcasts. In 2008, he started hosting the PGA's annual charity golf tournament—and it's now called the Justin Timberlake Shriners Hospitals for Children Open.

JT's own golf tournament—now that's a dream come true!

HOLLYWOOD JUSTIN:
Justin appears at the premiere of his movie *Alpha Dog.*

LIGHTS! CAMERA! ACTION!

Does Justin have what it takes to be crowned Hollywood's box-office king?

Singer. Dancer. Songwriter. Superstar. Everyone knew that Justin Timberlake was a man of many talents. In 2007, fans got to see their idol in a whole new light when JT made his debut on the silver screen. And he did it in not one but four films, if you count his role as the voice of Artie, the young King Arthur, in *Shrek the Third*.

Of course, acting was nothing new to Justin. He had done comedy skits in the *New Mickey Mouse Club*. But it wasn't until he appeared as a guest host on *Saturday Night Live* in

2003 that JT was taken seriously for his comedy skills. In one skit, he played Jessica Simpson—in a tight dress and a blonde wig. "He has great comic timing," *SNL* star Jimmy Fallon told *Rolling Stone*. "We were all impressed."

ON THE BIG SCREEN

Justin's 2006 return to *Saturday Night Live* made a similar impression on Hollywood's Jeffrey Katzenberg, producer of *Shrek the Third*. "[Katzenberg] said he saw me on *SNL* and was like 'That guy is funny; he has to play Artie,'" Justin told *Entertainment Weekly*.

Besides "voicing" his part in *Shrek*, Justin appeared in

small parts in three independent movies, all filmed during his time off from the music business. In the sci-fi flick *Southland Tales*, he costarred with Sarah Michelle Gellar and Seann William Scott. Gellar said that Justin buried himself in the role so well she didn't realize who he even was. "Seann introduced me to 'his friend Justin,'" Gellar told *Marie Claire* magazine. "He has no airs about him. And that's what you want when you do a film. You want people to bring clean slates and become these characters."

Director Nick Cassavetes worked with Justin in *Alpha Dog*, in which JT plays a bad guy. "If he wasn't so good," said Cassavetes, "the movie would fall flat on its face."

EASY AS IT LOOKS? Justin cracks himself up while recording for the blockbuster comedy *Shrek the Third*.

a natural

Justin played Christina Ricci's boyfriend in the film *Black Snake Moan*. Christina, who has been acting in movies almost her whole life, said Justin was a natural. "He could do things it took me years to do," she told *US* magazine. "I couldn't cry on camera for a long time. It's his second movie—and he does it perfectly!"

As soon as his 2007 tour ended, Justin went back in front of the cameras to film his hilarious role as a Speedo-wearing sleaze in Mike Myers's comedy *The Love Guru*.

By 2008, Justin had already branched out to become a Hollywood mover and shaker. In his first role behind the camera, Justin served as executive producer of NBC-TV's comedy series *My Problem With Women*. (Note to Britney and Cameron: Don't worry: Justin says the show is *not* autobiographical.)

T or F

?

Those are Justin's real tattoos in *Alpha Dog*.

FALSE! They're fakes that came off when he was done shooting.

CALLING THE SHOTS

Besides making movies, Justin proved to be a successful businessman. He launched his own music label, Tennman Records, as well as two restaurants in New York City. And when Justin wasn't feeding customers, he was outfitting them. He and his old friend Trace Ayala became co-owners of a successful clothing line.

With so much going on in Justin's life, it may have seemed to fans that their hero didn't have any time left for music. Then, in 2008, when word got around that the original boy band, New Kids on the Block, was regrouping, 'NSync fans began to get their hopes up.

Would the boys get back together for a reunion tour?

Since there could be no reunion without him, JT held the answer in his hands.

> He has some really emotional scenes where I think people will forget that it's Justin Timberlake. I did! We'd be doing a scene, and I'd think, "Oh my gosh, you were on the *Mickey Mouse Club!*"
>
> **OLIVIA WILDE,** *Alpha Dog* costar, to *OK* magazine

OVERHEARD

POP ROYALTY:
Justin has dominated
show business with
his looks, talent,
and humor.

FUTURE SOUNDS

For the pimply kid from Millington who wanted stardom, it's good to be the king.

Because 'NSync never formally broke up, fans have long hoped they would start touring again. Rumors first flew in 2004 when Lance Bass said the group was planning to record a new album.

Were the rumors true?

Justin had to be honest. "I think what we did doesn't work anymore," he told a reporter from the *Allentown Morning Call* in Pennsylvania. "I think it's kind of hard to make something work that was kind of a moment in time, especially when you're all such different people now."

ALL THE RIGHT MOVES:
Justin performs at the MTV
Video Music Awards.

Even if they never perform together again, the five band members are sure to remain good friends. In fact, Justin and JC Chasez still make music together. Justin helped produce JC's solo albums, *Schizophrenic* and *Kate*. JC never lets Justin forget who's older, but he has nothing but respect for his old friend. "The kid has stepped out!" JC told *Rolling Stone*. He added, "He's grown by leaps and bounds. He's a Jedi!"

aT THe TOP OF POP

The Force is definitely with JT these days. Some of pop music's biggest stars have lined up to work with him. Everyone from the Black Eyed Peas to hip-hop legends Snoop Dogg and 50 Cent have recorded with Justin.

In 2008, JT co-wrote and co-produced five of the songs on Madonna's album *Hard Candy*.

Madonna liked working with him so much that she asked him to introduce her at the Hall of Fame banquet.

T or F ?

Justin never graduated from high school.

FALSE! He attended school by mail during the first years of 'NSync. He graduated in 1998.

Somehow, when Justin wasn't singing, dancing, recording, producing, acting, starting restaurants, launching a clothing line, or running a record label, he found time to visit his family back home. "He always calls me when he's coming home and says, 'Granny, please don't forget my peach cobbler!'" Sadie Bomar told *People*. She used to send him batches of cobbler when he was on the road with 'NSync. He had to hide the goodies on his tour bus so the guys wouldn't gobble them all up.

WHAT GOES AROUND, COMES AROUND

Now, whenever Justin is in his home state of Tennessee, he catches up with his two half brothers, Stephen and Jonathan, as well as his father, Randy.

As for his mom, the two are as close as ever. Lynn, along with her husband, Paul, co-manages Justin's career. Justin's mom has sacrificed a lot to help her son pursue his dreams, and she likes to point out that Justin hasn't lost his gratitude. "When he was little," Lynn told *People*, "I used

CLEAR EYED: Justin has evolved from a teenaged heartthrob to become one of Hollywood's brightest young businessmen.

to say, 'Justin, someday when you get rich and famous, will you buy me a Harley?'"

Years later, after 'NSync first hit it big, Justin gave his mom a jewelry box for Christmas. Inside it were the keys to a new Harley-Davidson motorcycle.

SeTTLiNG DOWN?

As thrilled as Lynn and the family are by Justin's amazing success, they hope that he finds true happiness. His mom believes Justin will settle down one day and raise a family. "He's thought about what kind of father he wants to be," Lynn told *People* magazine.

But Justin's grandmother cautioned him not to rush into marriage. "I think he'll be a very loving husband, and when he makes that commitment, that will be it," Sadie told *People*. "For that reason, I'd like him to take his time and be sure of everything."

Good advice, Granny.

Justin himself can be sure of only one thing: "I'll never stop making music," he told a reporter. "But I do need a vacation now and then!"

JUSTIN

STAR GUIDE

Think you
know
everything
about Justin?
Keep reading!

STAR STATS

BORN: January 31, 1981

HOMETOWN: Millington, TN

SIGN: Aquarius

SIBLINGS: Half brothers
Jonathan and Stephen

HEIGHT: 6´2˝

SHOE SIZE: 11

EYE COLOR: Blue

HAIR COLOR: Brown

FAVORITE SPORTS: Golf and
basketball

FAVORITE COLOR: Baby blue

IS THIS JUSTIN?: No, it's a
wax statue!

1. **Justin was born in . . .**
   a) Kentucky
   b) New Jersey
   c) Ohio
   d) Tennesee

2. **Justin's grand-father used to play informal jam sessions with . . .**
   a) B.B. King
   b) Johnny Cash
   c) Elvis Presley
   d) The Beatles

3. **When Justin was really little and his parents would play music, he would . . .**
   a) sit on the kitchen counter and kick his legs to the beat
   b) use a hairbrush as a microphone and sing his heart out
   c) burst into tears
   d) play along on his toy piano

4. **Justin likes to wear a T-shirt that has which image on it?**
   a) Mickey Mouse
   b) the Hard Rock Cafe logo
   c) the Sun Studio logo
   d) "Got milk?"

5. **To convince his parents to let him pierce his ears, 14-year-old Justin . . .**
   a) pointed out that his mother had gotten her ears pierced when she was even younger than he was
   b) gave his parents an informative book on piercing customs all over the world
   c) wrote "The Earring Song" and sang it during a family vacation
   d) promised that he'd get straight A's

6. **Justin has a huge collection of . . .**
   a) Pez dispensers
   b) sneakers
   c) Happy Meal toys
   d) sunglasses

7. **'NSync recorded their first album in . . .**
   a) Amsterdam
   b) Tokyo
   c) Munich
   d) Stockholm

8. **Which of these is NOT a nickname Justin was called by his 'NSync bandmates?**
   a) Bounce
   b) The Baby
   c) Justice
   d) Curly

9. **In what surprising place did 'NSync sometimes perform?**
   a) cruise ships
   b) shopping malls
   c) Renaissance fairs
   d) schools

10. **Before launching their first solo American tour, 'NSync was briefly the opening act for . . .**
    a) Backstreet Boys
    b) New Kids on the Block
    c) Boyz II Men
    d) Janet Jackson

11. **Which of the following is NOT something Justin does when he needs to chill?**
    a) lights candles and meditates
    b) plays golf
    c) pages through his stamp collection
    d) retreats to his "Fun Zone," a room in his house with a pinball machine, an XBox, and a PlayStation

12. **Justin has reportedly dated . . .**
    a) Kate Hudson
    b) Scarlett Johansson
    c) Janet Jackson
    d) all of the above

TiMELiNE

JUSTIN

1996-97 'NSync tours Europe and releases its first album, *NSync*, overseas.

1998 'NSync becomes a hit in the U.S. Britney Spears opens for the band in concert and begins dating Justin.

1999 'NSync severs ties with its manager, Lou Pearlman, and records *No Strings Attached*.

1995 The *New Mickey Mouse Club* is canceled and 'NSync is born.

1992 JT loses on *Star Search* but joins the cast of Disney's *New Mickey Mouse Club* and moves to Orlando.

1992 Justin wins his first big talent competition in Nashville.

January 31, 1981 JT is born.

1989 Justin makes his stage debut at E.E. Jeter Elementary School talent show and then begins professional singing lessons.

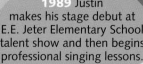

2007
Justin and Cameron announce their breakup. Justin stars in four films, including *Shrek the Third*, *Alpha Dog*, and *Black Snake Moan*. JT's second solo album wins two Grammy Awards.

2008 Justin inducts Madonna into the Rock and Roll Hall of Fame. He co-stars in Mike Myers's *The Love Guru*, is named executive producer of the NBC comedy *My Problem With Women*, and hosts ESPN's televised ESPY awards.

2006 Justin hosts *Saturday Night Live* again. *FutureSex/LoveSounds* establishes Justin as a darling of critics and fans. Justin tours Europe and continues to work on films.

2005
Justin begins recording a second solo album.

2004 Justin wins two Grammy Awards for *Justified*. He begins a two-year break from music.

2000 *No Strings Attached* becomes the fastest-selling album in pop music history.

2003 Justin begins dating Cameron Diaz. He launches his first solo world tour, makes his debut as host on *Saturday Night Live*, and is crowned "The New King of Pop" by *Rolling Stone*.

2001
'NSync's *Celebrity*, with six songs co-written by Justin, becomes the second-fastest-selling record in pop music history.

2002 The final 'NSync tour ends in Orlando, Florida. The band members announce that they are taking time off to pursue other interests. Justin and Britney break up. JT records his first solo album, *Justified*.

awards

Grammy Awards, 2004
"Best Pop Vocal Album"
"Best Male Pop Vocal Performance"

Emmy Awards, 2007
"Outstanding Original Music and Lyrics"

Grammy Awards, 2007
"Best Rap/Sung Collaboration"
"Best Dance Recording"

Grammy Awards, 2008
"Best Male Pop Vocal Performance"
"Best Dance Recording"

DiSCOGRaPHY

SOLO ALBUMS
Justified, 2002, multi-platinum
FutureSex/LoveSounds, 2006, multi-platinum

ALBUMS WITH 'NSYNC
*NSync, 1998, multi-platinum
Home for Christmas, 1998, multi-platinum
No Strings Attached, 2000, multi-platinum
Celebrity, 2001, multi-platinum

SINGLES
"**Like I Love You**," 2002
"**Still On My Brain**," 2003
"**Senorita**," 2003
"**Rock Your Body**," 2003
"**Cry Me A River**," 2003

"**SexyBack**," 2006
"**My Love**," 2006
"**FutureSex/LoveSounds**," 2006
"**What Goes Around . . .**," 2007
"**Summer Love**," 2007
"**Love Stoned**," 2007
"**Until The End Of Time**," 2007

TOURS

Justified, 2003
FutureSex/LoveShow, 2007

FiLMS

Edison, 2006
Alpha Dog, 2006
Southland Tales, 2006
Black Snake Moan, 2006
Shrek the Third, 2007
The Love Guru, 2008
The Open Road, 2008

NOTABLE TV APPEARANCES

Star Search, 1993, performing as Justin Randall
New Mickey Mouse Club, 1993–1995
Saturday Night Live, 2003 and 2006, as guest host and
  musical guest
Nickelodeon's 2007 Kids' Choice Awards, host
ESPN's ESPY Awards, 2008, host

Fan Sites

'NSYNC

www.nsync-fans.com

Visit this website for daily updates about Justin, Lance, and the other members of 'NSync. The site also includes online forums, photo galleries, and links to other 'NSync fan sites.

JUSTIN'S FACEBOOK PAGE

http://www.facebook.com/ justintimberlake

Get up close and personal with your favorite music star. Justin's page includes a message wall as well as links to YouTube videos, songs, ringtones, and more.

JUSTIN'S CHARITY
AMERICAN MUSIC CONFERENCE — STUDENTS PAGE

http://www.amc-music.com/advocacy/ students.htm

Check out this site to learn about the American Music Conference, a nonprofit that works closely with the Justin Timberlake Foundation to improve music education in schools.

more to read

Black, Susan and Justin Timberlake. *Justin Timberlake: Talking.* London: Omnibus Press, 2004. (127 pages)

Cefry, Holly. *Justin Timberlake (Contemporary Musicians and Their Music).* New York: Rosen Publishing Group, 2008. (48 pages)

Dougherty, Terri. *Justin Timberlake (People in the News).* San Diego: Lucent Books, 2008. (104 pages)

Heatley, Michael. *Justin Timberlake: Unauthorised.* London: Contender Books, 2003. (96 pages)

Marcovitz, Hal. *Justin Timberlake (Popular Culture, a View from the Paparazzi).* Broomall, Pa.: Mason Crest Publishers, 2007. (64 pages)

Roach, Martin. *Justin Timberlake: The Unofficial Book.* London: Virgin Books, 2003. (80 pages)

Tracy, Kathleen. *Justin Timberlake (Blue Banner Biographies).* Hockessin, Del.: Mitchell Lane Publishers, 2007. (32 pages)

Whitcombe, Dan. *Justin Timberlake (Star Files).* Chicago: Raintree, 2005. (48 pages)

GLOSSARY

ballad *noun* a song that tells a story

breach *noun* a failure to live up to a promise

charisma *noun* a powerful personal appeal

choreographer *noun* a person who creates and arranges dance steps and movements

contract *noun* a legal agreement between people stating the terms by which one will work for the other

demo *noun* an early recording of a performer or piece of music

devastated *adjective* shocked and distressed

ditty *noun* a short, simple song

diverse *adjective* varied or assorted

fanatic *noun* someone who is wildly enthusiastic about something

fleeting *adjective* not lasting long

harmonies *noun* sets of musical notes played or sung together as part of a chord

jam session *noun* session in which a group of musicians play together without any planning

liberating *adjective* allowing someone to feel set free

lip-synch *verb* to silently mouth the words of a song

negotiations *noun* meetings in which people who are opposing each other discuss things to come to an agreement

paparazzi *noun* photographers who pursue celebrities to get photographs of them

phenom *noun* slang word for "phenomenon," which means something very unusual and remarkable

promote *verb* to make the public aware of someone or something

sound check *noun* a test of sound equipment before a musical performance or recording to make sure the desired sound is being produced

tabloid *noun* a newspaper that has articles intended to stir up interest or excitement

JUNK FOOD

ABOUT THE AUTHOR

Steve Dougherty began his career writing about one Memphis favorite son, Elvis Presley, and caps it now by writing about another. In between, he has written about blues, jazz, country, rock and roll, soul, R&B, and hip-hop music and musicians for many publications, including the *Fort-Myers News-Press*; Gannett newspapers; the *Atlanta Constitution*; and the *Los Angeles Herald Examiner*. He is the author, with Ralph Cooper, of *Amateur Night at the Apollo* and *Hopes and Dreams: The Story of Barack Obama*.